I0158202

Mining The Diamond Within

7 Steps To Claiming What Has Always Been Yours

By: Benny Ferguson Jr.

Mining The Diamond Within

Mining The Diamond Within
7 Steps To Claiming What Has Always Been Yours
By Benny Ferguson Jr. © 2013

ISBN:
978-1-7354117-3-6

Published by: The Ferguson Company

Editing & Cover design:
http://roxanec.wix.com/time-to-read.com

Mining The Diamond Within

To assist you with realizing this connection, and to begin the process of Mining The Diamond Within, I offer these 7 steps.

These 7 steps place you in position to begin experiencing the life that you want. These 7 steps are proven and guaranteed to create improvements and/or changes in your life. You will know almost instantly that you are working in the right place. You will become aware of the tremendous amount of activity within your mind and body which conflicts and directly contradicts what you truly want to experience.

These steps have been discussed and outlined down through history. I have personally proven these steps to myself, and I constantly witness these steps at work in the lives of everyone around me.

A final note before we get started is, whether you know it or not, you are utilizing many of these steps right now. The challenge is that if you are not guiding them in the correct direction, toward the life that you want to experience, then you probably have them directing and driving you toward everything that you do not want.

So if you are ready, let's get started.

To Dos

- Pick one area of your life (relationships, finances, health, spirituality) to refer to for all exercises or to dos.

*Throughout this book you will have several (To Dos); these are short exercises that allow you to begin putting the steps into practice.

Congratulations on all of the changes and improvements that have occurred in your life by simply engaging and applying these 7 steps. I am proud of you.

Benny

Decide What You Want

"I want to be in a good relationship."
"I want to lose weight and be healthy."
"I want to earn more money."
"I want to be wealthy and abundant."
"I want to have a greater connection with Source."
"I want my life to be guided by strength and courage, and not by fear."

Well that's not good enough! These statements are lacking.

I have a friend (Craig) who is preparing to purchase his first home. He has looked at numerous houses but none of them have been quite right. Craig's challenge is that he does not know what he wants. What colors do you want in your home? How many bedrooms, bathrooms? How many stories? Where does it need to be located? Do you want a basement? How many cars need to fit in the garage? To get Craig started I suggested that, as he looked at houses and saw things that he liked, he began listing them. I suggested that he wrote them down to become clearer, more specific on what he wanted in a house.

The 1st step to *Mining the Diamond Within* is to decide **clearly** and **specifically** what you want. What type of relationships do you want? What type of finances do you want? What type of health do you want? What type of spiritual connection to Source do you want? What does it look like? What are the exact numbers? What are the exact colors? What are the emotions felt, displayed, and received? What are the behaviors displayed by you and by others?

This is the most critical step, because it grants you the idea, the image, the vision of what you truly want to experience and have manifest in your life. The completion of this step, establishes the background up to which all other steps are held.

To Dos

- Download Diamond Clarity Worksheet.

- Fill in the left side of the Diamond Clarity Worksheet with all of the things that you do not want and do not like, pertaining to the area of life you want to change or improve. Remember all of the stresses, all of the frustrations, all of the negative characteristics and attributes. This may take some time, but remember this is a process. You may not remember everything at the moment, but as the hours and days go by you will continue to be reminded of the details that you would like changed and/or improved.

- On the right side of the Diamond Clarity Worksheet, begin writing the absolute highest opposite of the statements on the left. This is the list of what you want to experience, the grandest experience that you can construct in your mind, and all of its characteristics and attributes. Write these statements in "I am …." format. There is much to be said about stating your desires in the present tense, but we will not get into that now.

Diamond Clarity

Diamond Clarity is an extreme level of specificity that grants you the necessary focus of mind to create the experience you want. As you become aware of the activity within your mind and body, you will find that most often you are thinking about, considering, entertaining images of, and repeating emotions based on what you do not want.

This is a magnificent focus, and to affect improvement and change, it must be curbed to what you want to experience.

Diamond Clarity places you in a powerful mental and emotional space because it places your awareness, attention, and focus on what you want.

This activity places you in a state of mind, a state of being that begins to mold you from the inside out, and to mold life itself in accord with your intention.

This is a critical step in reclaiming all of the beauty, the magnificence of life that is already yours. You must also remember that it is your responsibility to remain clear and to be led only by the images you have formulated in your mind of what you want to experience at every moment.

States That Keep You Stuck

Wishing is an idea of weakness and helplessness. You do not truly believe you can have it. You believe that there is someone or something that holds back your desire, and chooses whether you can have it or not, you believe that someone or something is choosing whether you are worthy of your desire or not. You do not believe that you have any responsibility in the matter. You actually believe that it is beyond your control.

Wanting is a slightly stronger state of mind. "I want to have better health." "I want to be in a better relationship." However, it still has the essence of not being responsible for the result, not being responsible for the outcome, not being responsible for whether it comes to pass or not.

Wanting is a nebulous possibility. When you say you want something, you think it is possible because you have witnessed or seen it in other people's lives, but you have not set a time frame, process or strategy for your desire to become reality.

How are you going to achieve or develop that loving relationship? How are you going to get fit and not be overweight? How are you going to make more money?

Wanting places you in a definite state mind, and it places your desires in a time and space that never comes.
.

To intend is the third and most powerful concept or state of mind. "I intend to be in a great relationship." "I intend to eat healthier and to be healthy." "I intend to make more money."

Intending centers you and sends more power through the mind and body. To intend for something to happen, means that you are taking some measure of responsibility for the outcome. To intend for something to happen, intend to achieve, to intend to be successful, for instance, means that you are taking the wheel. It means that you are taking control.

To intend means that you are going to have a definite time frame on the happening. You may not know how it is going to happen, but you intend for it to happen by a certain date.

You are going to do whatever you need to do, find out what you need to find out, gather the necessary skills, information, and resources to make it happen.

Intending is THE strength based idea. It must be the fundamental principle as you engage and approach your desires. To intend to have, to intend to achieve, means that you are taking responsibility for the outcome, and to decide and intend for an outcome is the first step.

Focus - "Shut Out The Clutter"

In Step 1 you became clear on what you needed to focus on. Now you must maintain that focus.

Step 2 in Mining the Diamond Within, Claiming What Has Always Been Yours, is Focus, and you have to shut out the clutter, all of the distractions that pull or drive you away from your desires.

The focus that we are discussing is an inward focus. It means becoming aware of all thoughts and emotions that contradict what you want to experience, you must notice them and simply let them go. You use them as triggers, as catalyst to remind you to focus on what you want. You use them as reminders to refocus, in mind, on the experiences that you want to have.

The critical factor of focus allows for all of the fears, doubts, and worries we have associated with our desires to be revealed. If you are paying close attention, you will notice that there are also physical feelings that manifest with them in certain parts of the body. It could be breathlessness, or weight in the stomach or chest areas. It could be an ache in the shoulders. All of these are proof of the existence of dominant ideas/unconscious beliefs you carry that conflict and contradict your desires. At present they stand between you and the life you want to experience.

Let's take relationships for example.

One evening my wife and I had some friends over for dinner. It had gotten late, we were all in the kitchen and the conversation moved to relationships. The ladies were explaining how they did not think that they would ever find a person to be in a good relationship with, much less get married.

I asked them, "When I say relationship, what comes to mind."
They said, "No good." "Not willing to commit." "Immature."

Mining The Diamond Within

One of the ladies said it reminded her of a past relationship. She described the pain that she experienced. She described and displayed the emotion that she experienced, and she said that she was trying to make sure that she never experienced any of that again.

After they finished explaining and describing what came to mind, based on the word relationship, I asked them a second question.

I asked them, "Do the thoughts, emotions, and behaviors that you display when thinking of relationships and attempting to protect you from pain in a previous relationship take you closer to or further away from the type of relationships you want to experience? Are those thoughts, emotions, and behaviors conducive to good relationship or not?"

I ask you the same question. "When you think of relationships, what thoughts and feelings come to mind?"

Do you begin to think of all of the experiences that you want to have, or do you begin to think of all your experiences from the past, the ones you are trying to escape from?

Do you truly believe in good relationships? Are they possible for you? Are they your reality, your normal experience, or are they just a faint thought, idea, or possibility?

Those ideas and thoughts that come to mind at the hint of your desire begin to reveal what you truly believe. The emotions and feelings that appear within your body tell the story of what you really believe.

Are your thoughts and feelings positive, exciting, and energizing about the experience of awesome relationships?

Or, are your thoughts and feelings negative, dark, and full of pain and discomfort? Are they the exact opposite of your desired end?

This is what your attempt to focus on what you want reveals to you. This is where the conflict exists. This is where the separation occurs. This is where the ideas reside, which will either move you toward or away from what you want.

On a normal, habitual basis do you think about what you want to happen or do you think about what you do not want to happen?

Every time you entertain ideas of what you do not want to happen or what you do not want to experience, you move away from what you want and you are attracting more of what you do not want.

But if you are thinking about what you do want to happen, and you are choosing to feel the emotions of that experience, then at that moment you are placing yourself in position to receive it. You are placing yourself in position to accomplish it. You are drawing the ideas, the resources, and the people necessary to make it your reality.

You do not begin to experience what you desire until you believe that it is possible for you.

You set out to achieve magnificent wealth. You want to increase your income by huge leaps and bounds, but all you have ever experienced is poverty and lack. You came out of a terrible relationship and want to experience a great relationship, but all you have had are strings of bad relationships. You have told countless others about these relationships. You are still passionate and angry about boyfriends or girlfriends that you had five, six, seven years ago.

You have experienced the pain numerous times. You believe in the experience of painful relationships, and it is your belief that has made it a normal experience for you.

You have to begin to shut out all of the things that take you out of alignment with what you want. The ideas, the thoughts, the feelings; you must begin to adjust them and direct them toward what you want.

Mining The Diamond Within

You are absolutely equipped and capable of doing it because they are just functions of the mind. This will work on memories. It will work on the past and all ideas that you believe to be true. Those ideas that you believe to be true in the unconscious depths of your mind are what you experience on a consistent, normal basis.

You say you want to be in a loving relationship, but thoughts of past pains are all that cycle through your mind. When you think about relationships, all of the names of the people, their words and behaviors come to mind. You project the thoughts and emotions you felt into the future so that you can protect yourself from experiencing them again, and with this happening your focus is constantly on what you do not want.

You have decided what you want. You have begun to shut out the clutter. You are using the ideas and thoughts that appear within you to trigger your focus on what you want.

You must begin to pay attention to what you allow to come into your mind.

Television, radio, and the problems and concerns of others all serve as input sources that are constantly creating or reinforcing dominant ideas or beliefs that you carry.

You must begin to be aware of the sources of media that you watch and listen to, and the discussions you engage in; noticing the messages that are implied.

Are the messages implying that stable, loving, caring, lasting relationships are possible and normal, or are they implying that broken, mentally and emotionally painful relationships are normal?

Do they imply that sickness and obesity are normal, or do they imply that purity and health are normal?

Do they imply that poverty, lack, and scarcity are normal, or do they imply that wealth and abundance are normal?

Mining The Diamond Within

Do you see great spiritual connection?

When other people declare to you their problems and concerns, do you hear belief in the good that is possible? Do they talk of great relationships? Do you hear talk of healthy choices and healthy possibilities, or do you hear talk of sickness and disease. Do you hear talk of opportunities, or do you hear talk of challenges and concerns?

All of the things that you allow into your mind are training you and teaching you what is true and what is possible? They are creating the ideas that you come to believe are true and possible for you. They are creating the ideas that yield your experience.

If you are going to mine for the diamond within, if you are going to mine for what you want to be true for you in your life, you have to begin to focus on what you want specifically. You have to begin focusing on what you want to experience in your life, and you have to begin shutting out the clutter. You have to begin shutting out everything that contradicts what you want to experience. You have to begin shutting out everything that presents ideas, thoughts, and emotions that contradict what you want to experience.

If someone is talking about terrible relationships, you have to shut it out because those ideas conflict with what you want to experience.

If someone is talking about terrible health, how diets do not work, and how it is difficult to exercise, they are presenting ideas to you that contradict your desired experience of a healthy mind and body.

You have to begin separating yourself, distancing yourself from any ideas, any habitual thought patterns; whether they are your own or other peoples that draw you away from what you want to experience.

Consider the implied message? Is it a message of success or failure? Is it a strength based message or a weak/fear based message?

Mining The Diamond Within

Think about what is being implied when you evaluate what other people say and what other people believe. Place what is being implied against what you now choose to think and believe.

You have decided what you want to experience. You are intending for it to happen. You are focusing only on those ideas, thoughts, and emotions that place you in alignment with what you want to accomplish, experience, or do. And, you are shutting out the clutter so that you can remain focused and in alignment with what you desire.

To Do

- Begin noticing all external inputs (conversations, radio, television). What is the implied message relating to the area of life you want to change or improve?

Attempt To Be That Person (You Forgot To Be)

Step 3 is that you must Attempt To Be The Person. This is the forgotten piece. It is the piece that is overlooked, left out, and completely missed by many systems of thought. It is the piece that is quietly present in traditions and teachings all around the world.

This step, clearly and directly stated, is that you must be the person that experiences what you want to experience in life.

If your chosen area to change or improve is relationships, and you say, "I want to experience loving, caring, fulfilling, fun relationships." You have to be loving. You have to be caring. You have to be fulfilled. You have to be fun.

The greater understanding and knowing behind being the person who experiences life the way you want to experience it, is recognizing that there are people who are already experiencing that life.

There is and have always been people experiencing the types of relationships you want to experience. And whether they know it or not, these people, to some degree, are being the type of person that experiences those type of relationships.

You can say that you want to experience great relationships, and you have never experienced great relationships in your life. All you remember is your mom and dad fighting and fussing. They got divorced or separated when you were young. You remember your mom or dad having breakup after breakup with different people. You remember hearing them arguing. You remember seeing fighting and a lot of conflict, and funny enough, you have experienced the same things in your relationships as an adult. There is always a lot of conflict. You have trust challenges. You do not really trust your partners. There are episodes of disrespect.

And so I ask you, "do the behaviors that you display place you in alignment with great relationships." Do the behaviors you display, in effort to protect yourself, place you in alignment with great relationships?

You cannot experience loving, beautiful relationships, and simultaneously be angry, disrespectful, jealous, envious, or any of those types of fear-based feelings or ideas.

They just do not go together, and you know it.

The truth of the matter, and which is written all around the world, is that you have to be that which you want to experience.

So if you want a loving, trusting, kind, strong relationship between you and another person, you have to be loving, trusting, kind, and strong.

If you want to experience increased finances, you have to be the type of person that experiences increase in their finances.

Nothing changes until you change on the inside.

So if you are making $30,000 a year now and you want to make $100,000 a year, you have to have the mindset of a person that makes/commands $100,000 a year. You have to be that person.

If you want to experience greater health in your mind and body, you have to be the type of person that experiences greater health. You have to be of the same passion and the same discipline for exercising, eating the right foods, getting the right amount of sleep. You have to be of the mindset of a person who achieves and lives greater health in their mind and body.

So step 3, to claiming what has always been yours, is to begin identifying the characteristics and attributes of those people who have already achieved what you want to achieve. You want to look around and find examples of people who are experiencing great health. What do they do? What do they think? How do they feel about eating properly? How do they feel about working out? You want to take on those characteristics and those attributes for yourself, so that in this area you can become like that person.

To Do

- Begin identifying the characteristics or attributes of people who are experiencing life the way you want to experience it.

Mining The Diamond Within

What are the characteristics and attributes of a person who is experiencing great relationships? Who are they in those relationships?

You have to take on the characteristics of those people who are already experiencing those types of relationships.

The bottom line is, if you were that person, then you would be experiencing those types of relationships.

Not only what they do, but what do they think? How do they feel about relationships? What do they believe to be true about relationships? Do they believe it is possible for them to have great relationships?

Obviously they do, because that is what they experience.

You have to take on those same ideas, those same characteristics, those same habits of thinking and feeling, and those same behaviors in order to experience the level of relationships that you want.

In doing this you have to remember that the mind yields behavior. Think about the fact that the person who has achieved great relationships does not have the same challenges as the person who is trying to have or find great relationships. You and the person who has great relationships do not have the same challenges or issues in relationships.

When you are focused and engulfed in your life experiences, you fail to realize that your best friend never has, or does not experience life the way you experience it. You have neighbors that do not experience life the way you experience life. So with that being known, you merely have to look to those people that are experiencing life the way you want to experience it and find out what they believe, how they feel, what they do or what their behaviors are that allow them to experience life in that area the way you want to experience it.

Mining The Diamond Within

The people that experience wealth and abundance do not have the same challenges as the person who is beginning to think about increasing their income.

The person, who has started multiple businesses, does not have the same challenges as the person who is looking to start their first business.

The person who has started multiple businesses is of a different mindset. They have experienced growth that has taken them far beyond the mindset and the experience of the person that is just starting out.

In your attempt to be that person, you have to consider and know how your choice of who you are affects others and affects the environment around you.

You have decided what you want to experience and you are intending for it to be so.
You have taken responsibility for it.

You have begun to focus on your desire and you are shutting out the clutter. You are paying attention to what you allow into your mind and body from television, from radio, from people, and you are noticing whether the ideas that are being presented to you are strength based or fear based. You are noticing whether they are placing you in alignment with what you desire and want to experience in your life, or whether they take you away from what you desire, and you are filtering that information.

You are beginning to choose to be that person. You are noticing what type of person experiences life the way you want to experience it. You are discovering what type of person experiences great relationships, dramatic increase in their finances, great health within their mind and body, and an alive, vibrant relationship with Source.

Mining The Diamond Within

Now, in the present moment, you are recognizing the characteristics, and are practicing being the person that experiences life the way you want to experience it.

Pay Attention to the Scramble and Challenge Your Ideas

Step 4 is to Pay Attention to the Scramble and Challenge Your Ideas. The only real problem is that you, on the inside, consisting of your dominant ideas/unconscious beliefs, thoughts, emotions, feelings and self-talk, do not allow and do not position yourself to experience the life you want to experience. If you did, you would be experiencing that life.

So now you are paying attention to the scramble, which are all of the things that occur inside of your mind and body that are in conflict with what you want. They are your habitual ways of thinking, feeling, speaking and behaving. They are also that inner chatter of disbelief, worry, and doubt. They are that inner chatter of whether it is possible for you or not, whether you are capable of handling it or not, whether you are capable of accomplishing it or not.

What we are talking about now are challenges of worthiness. Do you feel worthy of your desires? Are they possible for you? Can they actually be true for you? If you are asking can your desires be true for you, you must first examine, does anyone experience your desires. Does anyone experience the type of relationship you want to have? Does anyone experience the type of health you intend to have? Are they true; are they real anywhere in the world? If they are, they are possible for you but you have to begin to challenge the inner chatter in your mind. You have to begin to challenge the disbelief, the worry, the doubt that shows up as thoughts and emotion that stem that those ideas.

You have to prepare yourself with strength, and power based thoughts. If your chosen area of change or improvement is relationship, what are the thoughts and emotions that cycle through your mind and body when you meet new people or are having conversations? What ideas make themselves known in your mind? Are they ideas of opportunity, of possible relationship and possible awesome companionships, or are they ideas of broken relationships, of relationships not working out? Are they ideas and thoughts of

27

relationships and experiences from the past? If you are attempting to protect yourself from a certain type of behavior, then you are focusing on it and creating it in your experience. When you think about and feel the emotion of events that have happened in your past relationships, at those moments you are projecting them into your future. This is disbelief, worry, and doubt that positive relationships are possible for you.

So you are paying attention to the scramble. You are paying attention to the ideas that appear inside of you. You are paying attention to those thoughts and emotions, and they are letting you know what your unconscious beliefs are. They are letting you know the types of dominant ideas that are guiding your life, and when they appear, you have to have tools, you have to have thoughts and emotions that realign you and reposition you to what you want to experience.

Your inner representations, that inner conflict, how relationships are represented inside of you, how your finances are represented inside of you, how health is represented inside of you, makes all the difference, and you have to pay attention.

When you think about money, is it something good, or is it something bad? When you think about money, do you feel the feelings of lack and scarcity or do you feel the feelings of wealth and abundance?

You have to examine which types of ideas play in your mind when it comes to your desires, when it comes to those areas of life and ways of living that you want to experience.

To Do

- Sit or lie quietly, without movement. Consider the idea of the area of life you would like to change or improve. Notice the images, thoughts, emotions, feelings, and self-talk that arise inside your mind and body. Are they strength based or fear based? These are the results of the dominant ideas/unconscious beliefs that drive you in the area you have chosen.

Commit To Inner Growth and Change

Step 5 is Committing To Inner Growth and Change. You have to commit to inner growth and change long enough to begin to see the clearing. The clearing means that you begin to experience some of the things that you want to have happen. You begin to see things changing around you. Opportunities begin presenting themselves that you have not been aware of before.

This is the exciting part. This occurs when you have done all of the other steps and you are practicing. You are shutting out the clutter, all sources of information and ideas that conflict through the images, thoughts, and emotions that they cause you to entertain. You are continuously becoming clearer and narrowing your focus. You are expanding yourself on the type of person you need to be who experiences the life that you want to experience.

You have done those things and you are paying attention to the ideas that present themselves inside of you about the area you want to change or improve. You are paying attention to the ideas that appear, those normal thoughts, those emotions, and you switch them. You change them to ideas and thoughts that strengthen you toward what you want to experience.

Now you are committed to inner change and growth, and the clearing is beginning to appear. You are coming in contact with people who are able to help you along the way. You are coming in contact with people who are giving you advice and things that feel good when it comes to your desires. New opportunities are presenting themselves.

All of these events are directly related to the inner work you are doing in relation to the area you want to change or improve.

For example, you are starting to run into people and get ideas about how to be healthier, about eating healthier foods, on how to exercise in ways that would be fun for you. You are being asked to join exercise groups. You may find out your neighbor exercises 3 times a week and they have invited you to come.

Once you begin to intend. Once you shut out the clutter. Once you begin to work on being that person now, and you pay attention to the scramble and challenge those ideas by switching them when they appear inside of your mind and body, those old habitual ideas to new ideas that align you with your desired experience, and you commit to that inner growth and change, now the clearing and the evidence of your work are starting to appear. You are aware of it all because you are acutely focused on the activity and the work that you are putting in to claim your thinking and to command your mind, and to begin to be that person. You are noticing the clearing; you are noticing these things happening around you. You are getting a sense of the things that you can control. When you commit to inner change and growth you begin to notice what you can control in the matter when it comes to your health, your relationships, and your finances. The only thing that you can control is you and your habits, the habits of your mind. These are the only things that you can control. Nothing that happens outside of you, the people, the situations or circumstances, can you control. When something happens outside of you, as soon as it is manifest, it is history, and the only control that you have is your thinking, your emotion, and commanding and changing the ideas that guide you. This is the only control that you have.

You begin to realize that everything that comes and goes in your physical experience, everything that happens outside of you is not really you. It is an experience. It is an effect. It is not a cause. And, with your commitment to inner change and growth, with your commitment to be the person that experiences life the way you want to experience it, now you are taking control of the one thing that has always been our sole means for control, which is you on the inside. It should be your only major place of focus. You should only make sure that you are being that person, that you are commanding your habitual ways of thinking and feeling, and the dominant ideas that drive you. When you do this you are creating new pathways of choice inside of your mind and body. You are creating pathways to new opportunities and new experiences in your life.

Your experiences in life are merely effects, they are not causes.

When you commit to inner change and growth you commit to remaining congruent or in alignment.

These are beautiful words, congruence and alignment.

In this process you place yourself in alignment with what you truly want to experience in your life. It means you are staying focused, you are committing to noticing the chatter and separating yourself from all ideas, all sources that are presenting you information, whether they are other people or the media, that conflicts with how you want to experience life. You are gathering and taking on the characteristics and attributes of people who are experiencing life the way you want to experience life now.

In your relationships, finances, health, and spiritual connection with Source, you are committed wholly to inner growth and change, and you are beginning to experience and see the clearing, you are beginning to experience the attraction to people, resources, opportunities that are in alignment with what you want to experience, and not because you are working to stay in alignment, you are working to congruent with the life that you want to experience by being that person now through your thoughts, your emotions, and your behaviors, through commanding, changing or improving those unconscious guiding ideas until you get to # 6 where you now refuse to compromise.

To Do

- Create images, ideas, thoughts and self-talk that move you toward your desires. Switch to these creations anytime an image, idea or thought enters your mind that conflicts with what you desire.

Refuse To Compromise

In step 6, you are solely focused on the one thing that you can control, which is you on the inside, your inner condition. You are aware that there are no obstacles to your goals, to what you desire to experience in life until you perceive their existence. All obstacles appear first in the mind.

You have no obstacles to creating a $100 million company until you decide to build a $100 million company. The only obstacles that you can perceive in the initial are the obstacles that you have been told are there. So imagine that you were never told of any obstacles to building a $100 million organization or company, then there would not be any obstacles for you. You would drive forward, and everything that you needed to do, you would do. You would gather the necessary information, the resources, and you would continue to push forward, and manifest your business and your idea.

There are no obstacles in life until you perceive that there are, on the inside, and you must refuse to compromise with your desired experience. You must continually realign yourself with your desired experience. You are still gaining attributes and characteristics of the type of person who experiences the life that you desire so that you can be that person. You are paying attention to the chatter. You are challenging your present ideas with new ideas, with aligning ideas and thoughts that keep you congruent with your desired outcomes and you excitedly continue to realign yourself with your desired experience. You continuously entertain the image.

In the beginning you decided what you wanted to experience, and you intended for it to be so. You got Diamond Clear on what you wanted to happen. You got clear on the image and developed the idea, and you continually entertain that idea. You keep that image of what you want to experience in the front of your mind at every moment. You continue to see and recall that image. You see it as if it is in the present moment, as if you are experiencing it now. You are feeling the feelings and the emotions. You are seeing what would be happening, you are smelling any smells, and you are tasting any tastes as if it is present right now. You are staying aligned from the inside out.

When a person compromises they change directions in disbelief. They feel that the evidence of their imminent success or improvement is taking too long, or they are doubtful due to someone else's hint or suggestion or their own sabotaging self-talk.

What you must do in these cases, is continue to be aware of you on the inside. You must notice if what others are suggesting is taking you towards or away from what you desire. Are they aligning you with what you desire or are they causing you inner conflict. You must be constantly disregarding, replacing, and realigning yourself. In your not compromising, you remember that nothing is true for you until you believe it to be so. There is no experience until you believe that the experience is possible for you. You realize that all of this is a choice. It is a mental choice. Refusing to compromise with whatever area you want to change or improve is a mental choice. It requires knowing how to choose.

You must refuse to compromise, absolutely and wholly, refuse to compromise.

To Do

- Smile at all the ideas, thoughts, emotions, and suggestions which conflict with your desires, and then switch to the images, ideas, thoughts, and emotions of your desire. Experience them as if they are your true reality, your experience right now.

Realize Your Brilliance

Step 7 to Mining the Diamond Within, is to realize your brilliance. It is to realize that you are fully connected to something that is immense, and powerful. You are fully connected to the pure essence of life. It pervades you. It is you, and you are it.

You must recognize that you are connected to a Source that loves unconditionally, but at the same time is detached from your outcomes. You are the chooser of your life. You are fully connected to that which creates worlds. It is expansive, eternal, immense. It provides life to the animals, the trees, the plants. It exists in and through all of these things. It exists in and through you as an individual human being. There is no separation between you and life at its essence, at its core.

There is no separation.

Everything that you desire, everything that you want to experience in your life, you already have, you already are. The problem is alignment. The problem is the activity within your mind and body that has separated you from what you want to experience. This activity has you out of alignment with what you want to experience. Once you align yourself with it, it is yours.

Everything is available. Everything is possible for each and every human being. You are not separated from any person, from anything, from any idea. You are fully, wholly connected to magnificence, brilliance; there is no separation. The power of creation, to create, exists within you because Source, that which creates worlds, suns, galaxies is within you. It is you, and it empowers you to create your situations, your circumstances, your experiences, and the life that you want to have.

Once you align yourself with those experiences, you begin to draw and attract the resources, the environment, the situations, the circumstances for it to be true for you.

Mining The Diamond Within

Step 7 is realizing your brilliance, realizing your magnificence, realizing that your true power in life exists on the inside. Your true power exists in realizing that your life is being lived from the inside out, and that you must be proactive with your thought, proactive with your emotion, proactive with establishing the beliefs, the guiding/dominant ideas that guide your life. Knowing that your experiences are effects and not causes.

So one way to begin realizing your brilliance, that essence that resides in the depths of you now, is to use mental imagery. It is to use your imagination.

In quiet, imagine yourself at a favorite place. It could be a secluded beach, a quiet pasture, a hidden valley, a flower grove, any place that you hold sacred. A place that puts you at ease. A place that puts you at peace. Take a few moments daily. Sit or lie quietly and still, place yourself in those locations, and experience the peace, experience that strength, that inner power that resides within you. Experience that inner knowing that you feel once you quiet the senses and disconnect from the outside world. Once you have focused your awareness inward, and quieted the senses; realize the immense power, peace and potential that lie deep inside of you. Connect with it and allow it manifest itself through you. Allow it to move through every fiber of your being and into everything that you do. Cultivate and reside in that place, in that feeling. This must be established, cultivated and grown.

As I have stated, Mining the Diamond Within, 7 steps to claiming what is already yours are ideas, processes that are already at work. They are already in motion and will never stop from being in motion, the question is, are they guiding you toward what you want to experience or away from what you want to experience. Are your driving/guiding ideas ones of fear or ideas of strength and power? These are the questions. This handbook is a guide, an introduction to reclaiming your power and beginning to become aware of all of the things that are taking you away from what you want to experience. This handbook is a guide to recognizing that your life is being lived from the inside out. That cause and effect are definitely at work in every moment of your life, but the realizing is what is cause and what is effect. Life as you experience it outside of your mind and body is the effect. The causes are the activities that exist inside of you, the thoughts, the emotions, the driving ideas or beliefs that drive those thoughts and emotions, and are present and operate unconsciously. These driving ideas or beliefs are the fundamental causes of your experiences.

These 7 steps to claiming what has always been yours assist you in reclaiming that inner activity. Being clear and specific on what you want to experience in life:

- Shutting out the clutter, all those things that conflict with what you want to experience and cause conflict inside of you;
- Attempting to be that person, taking on the attributes and characteristics inwardly so that you begin to behave in a way that places you in alignment with what you want to experience;
- Paying attention to the scramble, noticing all of the ideas that conflict with your desires; and
- Challenging them, changing them the minute you are aware of them to strength based ideas that propel you toward your desires.

Commit to inner change and growth. Commit to practice and expansion in being aware of yourself and all of the thoughts emotions and behaviors that appear habitually, that are not in alignment with what you truly want. Notice the clearing, the information, the people, and the experiences that begin to show up and manifest around you that are in alignment with your desires and what you want to experience, and notice the frequency of appearances. Refuse to compromise your thinking and your feeling with any activity that happens in your life.

There may be a time lag between your experiences in the clearing. There may be a time lag for your desired experiences manifesting in your life, but you must refuse to compromise with what may be in front of you right now, refuse to compromise with your thinking and emotion and your guiding ideas, those beliefs that may be out of alignment. Continue to press and do not compromise with improving your inner activity because it is cause, and the life that appears in front of you are the effects. Realize your brilliance. This is the most powerful concept. Realize your brilliance. You are capable of all things now. You are worthy of all things now. Everything is possible for you now. Anything that has ever been experienced by another human being you can experience. There is nothing outside of you. There is nothing beyond you. There is nothing that you are not capable of. You merely must decide. You must align yourself. You must remember to be that person. And when you begin to align your unconscious beliefs, your dominant ideas with your desired experiences and you place yourself in alignment with those experiences, it is inevitable.

You must become aware that everyone does not experience life the same way. You want to experience great relationships. There are people out there that experience terrific relationships. You want to experience magnificent health. There are people who are in magnificent health. You want to experience wealth and abundance in your finances. There are people who experience wealth and abundance in their finances, and the only question to ask is, "What is the difference between you and those people?" There are people that experience a tremendous spiritual connection with Source. "What is the difference between you and those individuals?"

The only difference is in your mind, in how you think, in what you believe, and in what you believe to be possible for you.

These are the only differences!!!!

About Benny

Benny Ferguson Jr., once a weary traveler, feeling completely helpless to life, has suffered paralyzing fear, low levels of self-worth and depression, and contemplated suicide. He has attempted and failed, time after time, to achieve and succeed in his finances, his health, and his personal relationships, but always fell victim to unknown fears, self-sabotaging behaviors, limits and barriers.

His personal struggle culminated in 2005, with him waking up at 1:30 am in an anger rage. He woke up after a fear based dream, similar to the ones he had experienced dating back to elementary school. From that point he knew that there was more to life than he had previously been taught and ever knew was possible.

His search for an understanding of who he was, what he was capable of, and how to correct the unknown fears and barriers within, led him to the major spiritual traditions of the world (Teachings of Jesus, Buddhism, Hinduism, The Tao, Islam), branches of Psychology, and to Quantum Physics.

The Result:
"The Diamond Mind Approach....,"

where Benny ventures to explain and help human beings become aware for themselves (REMEMBER), that each individual is creating their own life experience through the images they hold as beliefs (unconsciously), their thoughts and their emotions.

Through acute observation, it is obvious that life is being lived from the inside out, and the moment we begin to live life from this understanding we realize that it is true.

Leadership ~ Organizational Culture ~ Customer Experience ~ Sales

"Maximizing Human Performance and Potential By Commanding the Mind"

Question: What is the most important part of an organization?
Answer: The individual

Question: Do processes exist and operate prior to skill and behavior?
Answer: Yes

Question: What are the lost/forgotten determinants to performance?
Answer: Inner workings of the mind

Question: What do these processes consist of?
Answer: Images/pictures, sounds, feelings, tastes, smells, and self-talk

Question: What is the most powerful choice?
Answer: A singular focus on desired outcomes with only consideration for their success

Mining The Diamond Within

Question: What is the result of this extreme focus?
Answer: Attraction of needed resources, acquiring of necessary skills; revealed inner blocks, revealed limiting ideas and beliefs that you hold about yourself, others, and what is possible

Question: Do I influence my life experiences and the successful completion or accomplishment of my highest goals and objectives?
Answer: Yes, all experiences are grandly influenced by their human participants

Question: Who is most influential?
Answer: The person who is most congruent or in alignment with their desired outcome

Question: Does the experience and performance of an organization have a determinant?
Answer: Yes, the cumulative mind and expectation of the whole

Question: Can the cumulative mind of an organization be controlled?
Answer: Yes, the continuous modeling and communication of the organization's purpose and vision by its Leadership, coupled with the continuous sowing of the images, in the team, of the behaviors and types of performance that yield the desired results

The Diamond Mind Approach...
E – Establish Ideal ~ P – Purify Mind ~ M – Master Senses

What You Learn, What You Gain:

- Learn to create ideals in and around your life, that dictate who you choose to be and how you perform

- Understand, become aware, and experience the processes at work within each human being that dictate behavior and performance

- Ability to dictate how you respond and behave in all situations

- Ability to program desired outcomes, and remain in alignment with them from the inside out

- Ability to identify limiting beliefs and emotions associated with undesired experiences

- Ability to call upon prepared and predesigned images that propel you into powerful mental and emotional states

- Release of stress, doubt, worry and fear

- Commanding presence and influence within your organization and abroad

- Heightened awareness to solutions

- Heightened creativity

*Each individual mind, crystallized around ideal experiences and results, accompanied with the necessary guiding ideas and beliefs dictates the behaviors necessary for powerful performance.

*Increased profits, exceptional customer service, and a powerful work environment are staples of an organization operating from the premise of a Diamond Mind.

About The Ferguson Company:

The Ferguson Company is emerging as a world leader in reminding human beings of their limitless power and potential.

Whether in an individual setting, as a business, or the grand operation of a large organization, the mind of the individual is the fundamental starting point to all behaviors and all experiences. **The inner workings of the mind are the Points of Power.**

Alignment is the lost consideration. In approaching desired outcomes, goals, and objectives, is the mind solely focused, through and through, on that end? Are the thoughts, emotions, words and behaviors of each individual involved in sync, in alignment with that end?

It is possible to cancel the clutter, release all limiting beliefs and ideas, and cultivate an inner, laser like focus that produces a level of performance that will not be denied. It is possible to claim results and outcomes before they appear in outer physical experience.

These are all forgotten attributes of the human being.

The Diamond Mind Approach is a guiding premise, with three comprehensive operatives:

E – Establish Ideals
Generate images of the most desired outcomes or experiences. Create these images in their most perfect form, engaging all of the senses.

P – Purify the Mind
Begin process of installing powerful, driving ideas and beliefs, while simultaneously becoming aware of and replacing all limiting ideas, beliefs and emotional blocks that are already present within the mind

Mining The Diamond Within

M – Master Senses
Recognize that all outer, physical experiences are effects and not causes. Therefore all less than desirable outcomes are no longer looked at as failure, but feedback. This feedback warrants inner adjustment, until the behaviors and performance that is displayed yields the desired outcomes.

Whether improved individual performance is desired, or the complete overhaul of an organization, *The Diamond Mind Approach* addresses the core foundation to behavior, performance and experience. *The Diamond Mind Approach* addresses mindset, the only area of a human being that precedes skill.

If you or your organization is truly ready to realize your limitless power and potential, then you must learn to master the mind.

Connecting With Benny:

Facebook: www.facebook.com/bennyrfergusonjr

Youtube: www.youtube.com/BennyFergusonJr/videos

Twitter: www.twitter.com/BennyRFergusonJ

Contacting Benny:

Initial contacts to Benny for discussions, interviews, one – on - one or group coaching, speaking or training may be made through telephone or email.

Phone: 336-546-7142

Email: BennyFerguson@TheFergusonCompany.com

www.ingramcontent.com/pod-product-compliance
Lightning Source LLC
Chambersburg PA
CBHW021920040426
42448CB00007B/842